Teen Voices
Real Teens Discuss
Real Problems™

Teens Talk About

Family Issues

Edited by Jennifer Landau

Featuring Q&As with Teen Health & Wellness's Dr. Jan

Rosen
YA™
New York

Published in 2018 by The Rosen Publishing Group, Inc.
29 East 21st Street, New York, NY 10010

First Edition

Library of Congress Cataloging-in-Publication Data

Names: Landau, Jennifer, 1961– editor.
Title: Teens talk about family issues / edited by Jennifer Landau.
Description: New York : Rosen Publishing, 2018 | Series: Teen voices: Real teens discuss real problems | Audience: Grades 7–12. | Includes bibliographical references and index.
Identifiers: LCCN 2017017630| ISBN 9781508176497 (library bound) | ISBN 9781508176572 (pbk.) | ISBN 9781508176336 (6 pack)
Subjects: LCSH: Families—Juvenile literature. | Dysfunctional families—Juvenile literature.
Classification: LCC HV697 .T44 2017 | DDC 362.82—dc23
LC record available at https://lccn.loc.gov/2017017630

Manufactured in China

The content in this title has been compiled from The Rosen Publishing Group's Teen Health & Wellness digital platform. Additional original content was provided by Anita Louise McCormick.

Contents

Introduction

The teen years are often a time of rapid change in family relationships. It is a time when young people are in the process of evolving from who they were as children into their new roles as adults. These changes come with new expectations and responsibilities.

Adolescence is a time when teens feel a growing need for independence and the right to make more of their own decisions. At the same time, they need their parents to be there to love, help, and support them as they go through the exciting yet challenging process of becoming adults.

Even under the best of circumstances, the teen years can feel like an ongoing balancing act. On some days, it can seem like whatever you do, someone will be upset. There are so many decisions to make about friends, school activities, part-time jobs, family life, dating, and upcoming decisions about college and careers.

It is also a time when young people start to think more deeply about their own identity and determine how their ideas and beliefs are similar or different from those of their parents. Ideally, families offer a solid ground of

Some of the most far-reaching decisions teens make involve career plans and education. Many teens visit numerous colleges and universities before making their final choice.

love and support for this period of growth and change. But in some instances, teenagers find themselves at odds with their parents when the religious, political, or other beliefs they want to explore are different from those they grew up with.

While all families go through challenging times, some issues such as adoption, divorce, difference of religious beliefs, or coming out as LGBTQ+ can be especially trying. While nearly all teens who were adopted know their parents love them, they often have questions about

Today's teens have access to ideas and opinions that are different from the beliefs they were raised with. Sometimes this can lead to conflict with parents.

their family of birth. When parents go through a divorce, it can leave teens feeling like their world is falling apart. And while coming out can be difficult under the best of circumstances, it can be even more challenging when parents or other family members are not accepting of the teenager's gender identity or sexual orientation.

Some issues, such as a family member having an accident or serious illness or experiencing a major change of income, can seem to come out of nowhere.

Share Your Own Story

The stories you are about to read were submitted by your peers to the Teen Health & Wellness Personal Story Project. Sharing stories is a powerful way to connect with other people. By sharing your story, you can connect with others who are dealing with these challenges. Find more information about how to submit your own story at the end of this resource.

They are often caused by factors no family member could have done anything to change. Yet, they can impact the entire family in ways no one could have realized until it happens.

Teens may struggle when trying to cope with these serious issues. Learning about other people's experiences and the challenges they faced can help readers understand the impact these issues had on their life, the emotions they felt at the time, and how they went about dealing with the problems.

Chapter 1

Teens Talk About Adoption

In this ever-changing world, it is common for teenagers to struggle with issues concerning where they belong in the family, with their friends at school, and in society in general. Many teens struggle with identity issues, such as the difference between who they want to be in life and what their family expects of them. When teens know that they have been adopted, these struggles are often intensified. Even if they were adopted as infants, teens who were adopted often wonder what their life might have been like if their birth parents had chosen to keep them.

Sometimes, having the opportunity to meet their birth mother and father brings understanding and closure. But in other situations, it only leads to more questions and brings feelings about being different or unwanted to the surface.

When the birth mother is from a different country, as is the case with transnational adoptions, questions can come up about differences in culture, ethnic identity, or spiritual beliefs. This can be an interesting learning experience for everyone involved.

Monica's Story

A picture of a dingy apartment complex and a Romanian flag hang on my bulletin board as a reminder of where I come from. I was born to an eighteen-year-old single mother with an eighth-grade education. I have no information on who my father is, and I have never met my birth mother. My adoption story leaves me wondering what my background is, what my parents were like, and why I was put up for adoption.

As a young child, I let my adoption define me as different and at times it had a negative effect on me. I felt disconnected from my family because I wasn't a blood relative and felt like the rest of them had their own personal connection that I wasn't a part of. I struggled and at times wished I had never been adopted and was still in Romania. These were many tough years, but as I look back I realize I was struggling because I didn't know who I was.

I am now seventeen. Three years ago, I traveled to Romania with my family. This was an eye-opening experience that changed my life and helped me understand where I was from. Romania's countryside was beautiful with rolling hills, men and women wearing traditional clothing, and cobblestone streets filled with wooden carts drawn by horses. I had a hard time believing that life was so hard for the orphans there. But when I reached the capital city of Bucharest, I was shocked by the poverty. The city was run-down and dark. You could see the remnants of communism in the decaying communist factories and in the bullet holes in the buildings.

Adopted teens who want to meet their birth parents from foreign countries such as Romania, shown here, may face additional challenges, including language barriers and adoption regulations that are different from those in the United States.

The hardest moment in my life, one that brought tears to my eyes, was looking out my hotel window and seeing a young boy staring up at me as he patted his belly and signaled with his hands that he was hungry. He was barely dressed, covered with dirt, and walking barefoot on the dirty streets. At that moment I realized I could have very easily been a child on the streets in Romania. I could have been sleeping on those streets and getting high off of spray paint in brown bags—a common sight throughout Romania.

Before returning home, my parents brought me to what they believed was my birth mother's apartment complex. Arriving at the complex, I was very emotional. The building was run-down, with chipped blue bars covering the windows and barefoot children playing soccer outside of the apartment entrance. I took pictures, walked around, and told myself that in later years I would return to meet my birth mother.

In the future, I plan to return, learn more, and hopefully meet my birth mother and visit orphanages. Romania's adoption program was shut down only a few months after I was adopted, but I hope it opens someday so that I may adopt a child.

Rebecca's Story

Why am I here? Why don't they want me? Why don't they love me? What would it have been like to stay with them? Where are they? Why do I feel like there's a piece of me missing?

Those are some of the questions children might have when they know they are adopted. For me, I don't remember ever not knowing I was adopted. I remember the story my mom used to tell me about how they came and got me from the Albuquerque hospital.

Then, when I was around twelve years old, we arranged to meet my birth mom. It was around Christmas. My family and I were staying at my grandma's house in upstate New York. My birth mom, mom, family, and I were going to meet her husband and her boys at an outdoor mall halfway between my grandma's house and where my birth mom lived. Before we even left Texas, I bought presents for my birth mom, her husband, and their little boy. We drove over two hours (all crowded into one car) and arrived right on time.

The mall was crowded and we had to drive around and around the parking lot looking for a space. While we drove, my mom tried to reach my birth mom on her cell phone. We were walking around and waiting in the cold December air. I think it was snowing. I was so excited because I would finally get to see who gave birth to me and maybe ask some questions. I would get to meet her husband and my little half-brother.

Hours went by. We kept walking and I kept looking into the face of each young mom who walked by. I thought, "Are you my mom? Are you my mom?" Each one walked by me, never even noticing I existed. So we walked around and waited. We were supposed to meet at the heart of the mall, in the food court. My mom kept calling and leaving message after message, but no call came back.

Pain, sadness, and so many questions ran through me. My mom wasn't happy with her. My dad was really mad. Why didn't she come? I wondered. Was she afraid? Did she not want to meet me?

We ate lunch, but I wasn't really hungry. I wanted the phone to ring. I wanted her to come. We finished eating, cleaned up, and then we were back outside walking around again in the cold.

We bought sneakers. I don't think we needed them. I think we just did it because we didn't know what else

When birth parents do not want to meet the teens they gave up for adoption, those teens may feel angry and rejected, and they may be left with many questions.

to do. Back outside it seemed colder and the light was starting to fade. After four hours of walking and waiting, my mom finally stopped it all and said what I already knew. She wasn't coming. We could walk all night in the cold, but nothing I could do would make her show up. No birth mom, no half-brother, and no other family—she didn't even call. She left me—for the second time in my life.

Finally, a few years later, I met my birth mom. It was an exciting experience. She lives in Long Island, New York. When we got there, her husband was so nice and warm and met me with open arms. My mom and I stayed there for a few hours. We brought my two half-brothers presents. At first, they were shy toward us. I was so afraid they wouldn't like me. Then they began to open up and started to get attached to me. I was filled with joy.

I took a ride in the car with my birth mom to see the new house they were going to move into. She told me I could ask her questions if I had any. I only had one. Why

When adoptive families and birth families get to know one another, they may find that they have many interests in common.

didn't she come to meet me that cold December day? She said it was because they were all getting sick. She didn't think it was a good idea to go in the cold.

She is a nice person. She and my birth father were not ready to be parents and were not married when they had me at nineteen. My birth father used to call my mom and check on me. Then he stopped when I got older.

When I tell people I am adopted they are like, "No way, really? You look like your mom." I find it kind of amusing because, at first, they don't believe me. I love my family. My parents truly care about me and love me. We don't know where my birth father is. My birth mom and her friends have been looking for him.

In my mind, the questions that were there are almost all answered. Why am I here? I am here because God put me here for a reason. Why didn't they want me? They weren't ready to be parents. Why don't they love me? They do love me. They loved me enough to give me to two loving parents who can take care of me better than they could. And they knew that. What would it have been like to stay with them? I wouldn't have the nice life I have now. I wouldn't have the friends I have or the good school I go to. Where are they? My birth mom lives in Long Island. My birth father? Unknown.

In the end, I am truly grateful that I am in this world. I think of how I could have not been born and not exist, and then I think of all the other people who are adopted. Some of them don't ever meet their birth parents. I am lucky to have the parents I have. I am happy that I can feel special because, yes, I am adopted, and yes, I have met my birth mom.

MYTHS **AND** FACTS

 MYTH   Adopted children often feel rejected.

 Many children and teenagers who were adopted feel grateful that their birth mother gave them a chance at a better life and that their adoptive parents chose to take them into their family.

 MYTH   When parents divorce, it means they will never get along again.

 Divorce means two people no longer want to be married to each other. But in many circumstances, they can eventually have civil and even friendly relations.

MYTH   If my loved one is diagnosed with cancer, it's a death sentence.

FACT   While each case is different, with proper treatment, many people diagnosed with cancer have a normal life expectancy.

Chapter 2

Teens Talk About Divorce

Dealing with a divorce in the family is challenging for teenagers in many ways. The situation can cause stress, feelings of anger and frustration, or even depression. Having divorced parents often means dividing time

When teens participate in sports or other activities, most divorced parents do their best to make sure the custody agreement allows their children to continue doing the things they love.

between the mother and father's house. Living this way can cause major challenges when planning for holidays and vacations, seeing friends from school on the weekend, and participating in extracurricular activities— especially if one parent lives in a different area.

For a teen, divorce can mean dealing with the strong emotions parents have about each other and the choices they make about new partners, moving to distant locations, and, sometimes, non-payment of child support. And divorce can mean being pulled between loyalties, especially if the parents have broken up recently.

When parents get a divorce, one of the most important things for a teen to remember is that the divorce is not his or her fault. It is because of issues between the parents, not because of anything the teen or his or her siblings might have done.

Christina's Story

I am seventeen years old and my parents are divorced. They divorced when I was two or three, so I do not really remember it. I live with my mom and stepdad. Every other weekend I go to my dad's house. So, every other weekend I have to pack a bag and bring all my schoolbooks to my dad's. Sometimes I get frustrated, because I don't like having to pack everything up and leave one home for another.

Even though I know it is not possible, I still wish my parents were together. I see my friends' families that are still together and long for my family to be like that. While

Teens who have divorced parents often have to deal with living in two different locations. This can lead to resentment and the feeling that they don't have a real home.

I am doing homework, I do not enjoy having to call my dad and ask him how to do something over the phone. When I watch TV or go out, I see families laughing and having a good time. Although my parents fight a lot when they talk, sometimes they can be civil. I am usually the one doing all the talking when the three of us are together. I have to ask one parent a question, get the answer, and repeat it back to the other.

Although having divorced parents is horrible, there are some positive sides to the situation. If I get tired of staying with one parent, I can go over to my other parent's house for a while. When I go over to my dad's house, I get a break from being at my mom's. I like being able to go over to my dad's house because he is more laid-back than my mom. However, my parents' houses are on opposite sides of the city. My mom lives next to a lake and my dad lives in a closed community. It is like having two different homes. I have two completely different rooms that I really enjoy staying in.

When I was three, I never thought I would have divorced parents. I have decided when I grow up and have kids of my own, I do not want to put them through what I went through. I do not want them to deal with all the terrible things that come with divorce. In having divorced parents, I have learned that not everyone can get along, but somehow they must find a way to cope with their disagreements.

Allison's Story

I was two years old when my mother divorced my father. My memory of that event is blurry, but I know that my sister, who was six at the time, cried often out of confusion. We were all living in Bridgewater, New Jersey. But when the divorce was filed, my mother, sister, and I picked up our belongings and moved to Livingston, New Jersey, where I have lived ever since. Growing up with divorced parents has shaped how I view my world.

I think of my father as the man who helped create me. The title "father" does not fit his role in my life. He lives about three hours away by plane and eighteen hours by car. I don't see him very often, nor is he someone I would enjoy spending time with. When I was growing up, my father criticized me for the way that I looked: my weight, my height, and even my hair color. When I visited him, I ran laps, even at only five years old, and ate only two times each day. He was trying to shape me into something I was not ready to become—thin. I felt jealous of how he praised my sister for her beauty. I could never live up to that. I cried to my mother to let me skip the visits. He yelled at me for getting a C in my third grade English class. I have a learning disability, something he has never quite understood. My relationship with him reminds me of the energy between two magnets: there is a connection between the two, but somehow one doesn't seem to want the other. Although I have a father who treats me poorly, I am confident that the men who will come in and out of my life will be nothing like him.

My relationship with my mother could not be more different. I love talking about my mother. She is my personal Wonder Woman. When I was diagnosed with ADHD, she helped me through it all. In elementary school, I would cry when I had a hard time staying focused. The other students called me stupid, ugly, and retarded. But when my mom gave me a hug and said, "Everything will be okay, honey," she made me feel better—safe and loved.

In some cases, a teen spends a majority of the year with one divorced parent and has infrequent visits with the other. This often happens when one parent lives some distance away.

My mom is a highly accomplished lawyer and works hard every single day to support our family. I never minded having nannies come through my life, because each day I know that my mom puts on her Wonder Woman outfit and battles annoying, criminal people. It is amazing how our relationship has turned out. We don't fight very often and when we do fight, it is usually over something very little. I make her feel better after a long day at work and she makes me feel better after a long day at school.

As I become a young woman, I want to grow up to be like her. She has taught me to not put on a mask, but to open myself up and bring in the people who like me without my mask. I have never felt pressured to be the perfect child and student because she knows that she, herself, is not perfect. She is proud of me for just being me. Our magnetic pull has a strong energy that is almost dreamlike. Hearing her coffee brewing at 6:30 a.m. is just what I need to start my day.

After a divorce, a teen may feel more closely connected to one parent. Spending time with that parent can offer comfort during a time of stress and upheaval.

My parents' divorce was the best and worst thing that ever happened to me. I may have one absent parent, but I have an amazing other parent. In some ways, I am almost grateful for this situation because I got to understand both of my parents more deeply. Down the road, I know that if my children need help, I will put on my very own Wonder Woman outfit and help them however I can.

Chapter 3

Teens Talk About Illness in the Family

Illness can impact families in many ways. A sudden or serious illness in the family often causes a teen to feel like the world is falling apart. One day everything seems to be fine; then suddenly a disease or accident strikes a family member, friend, or classmate, and the well-being or survival of someone they love is now in question. This hardship often causes teens to feel fearful about not only the health of the person dealing with the illness, but also the possibility that something bad might happen to other people they care about.

Serious illness often changes the roles teenagers play in the family. They might be asked to take on new responsibilities (such as caring for younger brothers and sisters) while a parent is recovering or needs to spend time at the hospital with a sick family member. Family illness can mean giving up after-school activities, such as sports or clubs. It can also mean that money is tight because of medical bills or because the ill person is not able to work.

While dealing with serious illness can be quite stressful for the entire family, many teens look back on

When coping with a loved one's illness, family members often rediscover the joy of doing simple things such as reading a book or watching a movie together at home.

the situation as a growth experience that helped them feel more mature and confident that they could deal with whatever life throws at them.

Brittany's Story

I started out my school day like any other normal school day. I went to my regular classes and got the same old homework and writing assignments. Then lunch came around. I was sitting at lunch eating my usual salad, pizza, and baked BBQ chips. I looked up from eating and saw my mom standing in the hallway outside the lunchroom. "Mom?" I thought, "What is she doing here?" As I walked toward the door I could feel the hair on the back of my neck begin to stand up, my heart rate increased with every step closer to the door. I could not understand why my mother was at school.

When I finally got to where she was standing I could see something wasn't right. Her eyes were bloodshot and puffy, and as she stood, she seemed very unsteady.

"What's wrong? What are you doing here?" I asked.

"It's your father. He has been rushed to the hospital with internal bleeding in his brain. The doctors are deciding whether to do emergency brain surgery or not. I'm flying out to Mississippi to be with him. Stay here and stay concentrated on school. I will call you when I know something else," she said quietly.

I stood there for a moment just staring at my mother. I wanted to say something, but I couldn't get words to come out. It was like they were stuck to my tongue, like my tongue was made of glue or something. It wasn't even a lot of information, yet I had the hardest time comprehending all of it. Was she really just expecting me to stay put and not worry? I can't just stay here, I thought, but what else could a seventeen year old do? My mom kissed my forehead, told me she loved me, and told me to behave. I still just stood there in silence. Was this really happening? Was my father going to die?

I still had things I had to do at school so there was no point in dwelling on the situation. But that was easier said than done. When I tried to focus on school, I

When a family member has a serious illness, a teen may be so worried about his or her loved one that it becomes difficult to focus on schoolwork.

couldn't. When my teachers lectured, their mouths were moving, but I couldn't hear anything. I couldn't stop thinking about the two-minute conversation I had with my mom just forty-five minutes earlier. My two other sisters called me, crying hysterically, asking for my help. I told them both to be calm, that everything was going to be okay, and that they had nothing to worry about. I could feel the pressure of the world on top of me, and my legs were starting to crumble beneath it.

I usually have a high tolerance for stress, but not this time. I knew I couldn't handle all this on my own. If it wasn't for my friends I wouldn't have been able to keep my emotions under control. My father ended up having emergency brain surgery and after a couple months, he recovered quite nicely. My advice to others with stress: Just remember to not think the worst, and everything will be okay in the end. No matter what.

Brielle's Story

After only eleven short years my cousin Michael was told that his time on earth was limited. In December of 2005, Mikey was diagnosed with one of the rarest cancers known. It was a type of blood cell cancer, and his diagnosis left everyone in a state of complete shock. Why Mikey? What did he ever do to deserve this kind of pain and hardship so young in his life? Our minds were full of unanswered questions. The day the news was delivered will forever be one of the worst days of my life.

Mikey was always the outgoing, funny, free spirit in our family. He never complained and was always willing to "go with the flow" or please everyone else, even if it meant not pleasing himself. Michael, his brother Justin, my aunt, and my uncle moved to California when I was extremely young. Growing up, I was always close to Justin because we were around the same age, and Mikey was always the cute little cousin who we never minded having around.

The only thing that gave the slightest justification to this terrible time was that the world is a cruel and unfair place, and Mikey knew that. He immediately started visiting the San Diego Children's Hospital frequently. I occasionally talked to Justin during the first couple of weeks of Mikey's diagnosis. Nothing was getting easier for anyone, including me. One afternoon my phone rang and up popped the adorable face of my cousin on the caller ID. I answered with anticipation, excitement, and fear. On the other side of the call was a voice with hidden sadness. I could tell that Mikey wasn't his normal self, and that absolutely killed me. He asked me if there was any way I could come to San Diego to see him. The next morning, my mom dropped me off at the airport, and I was on my way to California.

After my aunt's assistant picked me up, I went straight to the hospital. I opened the door to an unfamiliar room to find an unfamiliar boy lying on the bed. Mikey had lost his hair, his smile, and his spirit. The next three days were filled with laughter and heartache.

I stayed at the hospital day in and day out. When I was taken on a tour of the colorful floor at the local Children's Hospital, Mikey not only showed me the ins and outs of every room but also introduced me to every

Offering words of encouragement to a sick friend is one of the best ways to keep his or her spirits up.

nurse, doctor, and patient there. It was at that moment that I realized that my cousin was still there. He might be bald, have a different blood cell count, and a couple more scrapes and bruises, but Mikey's true inner self would never fade.

Those seventy-two hours changed my life.

From then on, I would go see Mikey every chance I got. By the end of his first chemo treatment, I had visited him eight times. We had become closer than I will ever be with anyone. He told me secrets that will stay with me forever.

I was there for the good days and the bad days, the frightening and positive words from doctors, and countless tears and smiles. After one fairly good weekend with Mikey, my mom picked me up from the airport with a quizzical look on her face. She told me that the cancer was spreading, but the doctors were doing everything in their power to stop it. At fourteen, I figured that was the easiest way for my mom to tell me that my cousin might not be with us for much longer.

Throughout all of this, I never heard one single complaint out of Michael. He was the definition of strong. Toward the end of the battle, we started going up to visit Mikey as a family. While my aunts, uncles, and cousins were surfing, eating, and spending time with each other, I was in the all-too-familiar hospital room. Little did I know that was the last time I would ever see Michael suffering in a hospital room.

As quickly as it all started, it ended. Only the news that we were given was different this time. After two years of fighting, Mikey was finally cancer free. Contrary to so many beliefs, he had beaten it.

If you ask him now, he will tell you that having and overcoming cancer has made him a better person. Now every morning Mikey wakes up, counts his blessings, and goes surfing. Never in a million years would you walk by this average fourteen-year-old boy and know what he had been through so young in his life. Michael will forever be my cousin, my best friend, and my hero.

Ask Dr. Jan

Dear Dr. Jan,
My parents fight a lot and sometimes I wish they would just get divorced. It's hard to live with so much yelling and tension. What should I do?
— Kylie

Dear Kylie,

Living in a household with yelling and tension is a very toxic environment for everyone. While it is important to let your parents know that their behavior is very disturbing to you, it is equally important to realize that only they can change their behavior, not you.

What you can do, however, is take care of yourself. In situations where we cannot change the things that are painful and disturbing to us, the best way to feel better emotionally is to get those feelings out in healthy ways. In addition to letting your parents know how you feel, release those feelings through writing, art expression, or talking to a trusted friend.

If these efforts are not successful, speaking to a professional can be of great value. A school counselor can often be a great place to start. This is particularly true if your family is experiencing physical fighting in addition to arguing.

While it is often difficult to "fix" our family, it is always a good idea to take care of our own emotional well-being.

Chapter 4

Teens Talk About Family Conflict

The teen years are a time of growth and self-discovery. It is natural for teenagers to question many things about life and the world they live in, including their parents' ideas about school, career choices, sports and other extracurricular activities, music, dating, plans to move away and attend a distant college, or even joining the military.

It is also common for teens to question the religious beliefs of the family. The act

Although the military offers educational opportunities and a chance to serve one's country, many parents worry that their son or daughter might be sent into dangerous combat situations.

of questioning these beliefs can put teens at odds with their parents, especially if they grow up in families where only one set of ideas about religion is deemed acceptable.

It can also be very difficult for teens growing up in strict religious families to talk to their parents when they discover they are gay, lesbian, bisexual, or transgender. While there are many resources available to help LGBTQ+ teens, it can be a very stressful time if parents are not supportive.

Gabriella's Story

Throughout my entire life, I have been raised as an Orthodox Jew. I did not have a choice on whether or not I wanted to be Jewish. I had to be. My family had carried their Jewish heritage throughout centuries, and I was counted on to continue the tradition, as well. They founded the Jewish community in my hometown. My grandpa, a Holocaust survivor, was more determined than ever to keep his religion alive. He did so by establishing a Jewish day school as well as a synagogue. He has been praised for his philanthropy and dedication to the Jewish community. Now, because I follow in his lineage, am I supposed to carry that same passion, love, and dedication that he had towards Judaism?

As a child I always went with the flow. I had no complaints because I did not know there were other options. Originally, I began my schooling in the same school my grandpa had built. I stayed at that school until I was diagnosed with a learning difference. My parents

Religious ceremonies such as a Passover seder are often observed throughout many generations. But some teens brought up in a certain faith choose to veer from that path as they get older.

willingly placed me into a school where they knew I would be successful. They sent me there knowing they would have to face the disappointment of family members and aware that I would not receive a strong Jewish education, something very valuable to my family. I was unaware of what was happening and continued to follow my parents' lead, obeying what they said. To make up for my absence of Jewish education, I was sent to a tutor, who exposed me to an in-depth study of my religion. She helped me feel more a part of my culture, but I still never developed the confidence that allowed me to become fully accepted in my multi-generational Jewish family. I remained an outsider.

In school I was different because I was an Orthodox Jew and in temple I was different because I did not attend a Jewish school. There was no place where I truly fit in. I felt as if I was living two different lives that had two different visions. At the time I was not aware of the emotional damage that was being inflicted upon me and did not realize the pain and stress of living two intersecting lives.

As I entered high school, I felt the emotional burden of my two lives and saw that they did not connect with each other in any way. I tried to make them interact with each other, but every time I brought part of one life into the other I would lose something I loved—either a person or a passion. I remember the pain and pressure was so difficult. I was hurt deeply. I did not understand why someone's religion could be in such conflict with their life. I always thought religion was supposed to help; it was something you turn to when in doubt. However, instead of turning toward it, I turned away from it.

Now I am scared that because I cannot believe in Judaism, my family will not accept me at all. I do not get it. I am a great student with good intentions, but still, because I cannot find it in me to accept Judaism, my family will not accept me. That does not make sense. It is a lifelong battle for me to fight through. However, from this experience I learned that life is a puzzle composed of many pieces, but sometimes not all those pieces fit together.

Matthew's Story

Growing up is always hard. It takes work to discover who you are, what you like, and to become independent, all while trying to conform to the perceived standards of society and your family. When I realized that I was gay, my whole life came tumbling down around me. All through middle school everyone had always called me names like gay or fag, but I just thought they were kidding or giving me a hard time. How could I be gay?

I was raised with the very conservative mentality that being gay was wrong and a sin even. Yet at the same time I had always known that I was attracted to men. I gravitated toward girl friends because I was always much more comfortable hanging around girls than guys. Yes, I did have guy friends, but it just wasn't as natural. When I was six, the only present I asked to get for Christmas was the Barbie RV set. But my mom said boys don't play with Barbies. Instead, I just played with my friend Sarah's Barbie airline set.

Until the sixth grade, I didn't even know there was a word for men who liked men. My family always used the word gay as a bad thing, like people who were gay had something wrong with them. All through middle school I became numb to people calling me names. While it hurt, it hurt less if I just paid no attention to it. Only in seventh grade did I begin thinking, "What if they are right?" Then I realized that I was gay; it was my deepest, darkest, ugliest secret.

I thought that everyone would hate me if they knew what I was. By this time, I had absolutely no self-esteem

Although being LGBTQ+ is more accepted today, teens can still be ridiculed because of their sexual orientation or gender identity.

and held people at arm's length from my true self. I tried to be exactly like this person, or that person, so no one would know the real me. I would think of ways my family would never have to know my secret. I could marry a woman so everyone would think I was straight. Or, I could just never marry and live my life alone. I finally told one of my friends in seventh grade. For three years she was the only one who knew. The closet is a poisonous, suffocating place. I was still a self-loathing person until the end of eighth grade, when I realized that it didn't have to be so bad. Gay people aren't awful people like I was taught to believe.

When I was a freshman in high school my mom started talking to me and telling me how bad being gay is. She would always bring it up in the morning in the car on the way to school. She said that America would pay the price if they gave the gays the right to marry. She, of course, was talking about God and his hatred for gays. I prayed every day, sometimes multiple times a day, that God would just take this thing out of me. I didn't want to be this way. Why did I have to be so different? I just wanted him to make me normal or kill me already.

I finally started coming out to my friends and was still not sure if I was comfortable with myself of not. As I came out more and more it became less stressful. I remember that I thought it would be the end of the world if one of my friends told someone. My freshman year I met a senior named Alec and he became what I jokingly called "my gay mentor." He talked to me about coming out and being comfortable with myself. I probably wouldn't be the same without him today. Sophomore year, I was out to many of my friends, but still not publicly. I still remember when I became comfortable with coming out to everyone. Someone asked me if I was gay and I said, "Yes, but how did you find out?" He simply told me that his friend Ben in his advisory told him. At that point, I was astonished that Ben hadn't acted any differently towards me after finding out that I was gay.

No matter what challenges a teen may be facing, having friends and mentors he or she can depend on for support makes it far easier to deal with those struggles.

I asked him why, and he just told me that I was "still a cool guy."

At that point, I realized that if my friends stop liking me, then they were never really my friends in the first place. My best friend from middle school told me never to talk to him again, which hurt, but if people don't want me in their life, that's not my decision. I also became good friends with my librarian, who helped me be more

WHOM TO CALL

The following hotlines and organizations offer support for those dealing with a variety of family issues:

Al-Anon/Alateen
888-425-2666
http://www.al-anon.alateen.org/index.php
8 a.m. to 6 p.m. EST, Monday to Friday

GLBT National Youth Talkline
800-246-PRIDE (7743)
http://www.glnh.org/talkline
4 p.m. to 12 a.m. EST, Monday to Friday
12 p.m. to 5 p.m. EST, Saturday

Crisis Call Center
800-273-8255 or text ANSWER to 839863
http://crisiscallcenter.org/crisis-services
Twenty-four hours a day, seven days a week

Thursday's Child National Youth Advocacy Hotline
800-USA-KIDS (800-872-5437)
http://www.thursdayschild.org
Twenty-four hours a day, seven days a week

comfortable with myself. She was also a great mentor and ally for me to fall back on when I was still unsure about coming out.

If I had to give one piece of advice to anyone, gay or straight, it would be to love yourself and not take to heart what anyone else thinks about you. Homosexuality doesn't define a person, so don't let it become a deciding factor in whether or not you make friends with someone.

Chapter 5

Teens Talk About Family Challenges

Having to deal with major family challenges is never easy. Often, these challenges result from larger situations, such as a downturn in the economy, that no one in the family could have done anything to prevent.

When a mother or father is in jail, a teen can experience many feelings, including anger, loneliness, and the fear of being abandoned.

If a parent who has served in the military is unexpectedly called back and deployed to a distant country, every member of the family is called upon to deal with the changes this situation creates. Another major family challenge some teens face is when a parent is convicted of a crime and sent to jail.

When a family challenge prevents a parent from providing the level of income the family is used to, it often means giving up things like vacations, extracurricular activities, eating out, and concerts, and sometimes even basic needs, at least until things get better. Otherwise, there won't be enough money for housing, food, and transportation. When this happens, parents often give up at least as much as they ask their teenagers to sacrifice.

One way teens can help is to get a part-time job to pay for special things they want and contribute to the household income. Even if the only part-time job teenagers can get has nothing to do with their career plans, it can help get the family through a difficult time and be valuable work experience to add to their resume.

Libby's Story

Having one of your parents live in a different state is hard, especially when your parents are still married. In order to work, my father has to live in a state seven hours away from us. He comes home every three or four weeks, stays for three days at most, and then leaves to go back to his job. He sleeps a lot when he is home, so I don't talk to him much. My mother talks to him every morning on the phone, so we often communicate through her. The emotions that come with this lifestyle are brutal on the whole family.

The worst part is explaining it to friends. They don't understand. They don't get what it is like to be a seven-year-old girl, happy as can be, and then all of the sudden Daddy comes home after being gone for a week. Then he is ripped away from her just three days later. My father used to get so mad at me for crying when he left. I think it's because my tears felt like bullets to his heart and knowing that he made his daughter cry could make just about any man feel awful. When I was little, no matter what holiday came up— Christmas, Easter, my birthday—all I would ask was that Daddy stay home for a week. I never asked for anything else. Not a pony, or a puppy, or a tiara. Just for my father to be home.

During a difficult economic period, a parent may have to take a job that requires him or her to be away from home more than the family would like.

I often got mad at my father for leaving on business trips. I thought he didn't care about me or my feelings, and that work was more important. But he had to take the job. When he first started, he didn't know he was going to be gone so much. He told me that his contract ended at the end of my sixth grade year of school and he would be home for good after that. I use to count down the days, hours, and seconds until that day because I just wanted to have a normal family with a daddy, a mommy, a sister, and me. But alas, my father hid from me that he renewed the contract, and we were sent back into the vicious cycle. My father had to do this, though. It was the only way he could support our family. He didn't make enough money working in our hometown—the big bucks were seven hours away! It was either have the money to support our family or have little money and have a dad at home. I would have been happy with the second option, but the first one was more practical. I believe that my father made a good choice.

It has been seven years since my father started taking business trips all the time. People still don't understand it. It is hard to live through. But it has made me stronger and taught me to cope with things, even when no one understands. I try to help others when no one knows what they are going through as well because I know that feeling. I hope someday my father and I can have some quality time together, maybe after he retires. The future is uncertain. We just have to hope. I love you, Daddy.

Arlene's Story

One day, Betty and I were recollecting about our middle school trip to Florida. We had gone snorkeling in the Keys and swimming among the fish and coral reef. It was an amazing experience with the sights and the smells, the quaint cabin, and the expansive sea.

Andrew interjected, "I wouldn't know. I didn't go. It was too expensive."

A silence emerged, followed by a change in subject. I felt sympathetic, but couldn't relate. Both my parents had doctorates and worked full-time. My family had always been financially well-off. I knew Andrew lived with his single mother who was an elementary school teacher, a respectable but low-paying job.

Talking about family income was socially acceptable, wasn't it? It's about your parents, so you shouldn't take offense. But what did I know? I was a thirteen-year-old girl who just learned what "mortgage" meant.

I was a teenager with a few simple demands that were almost always met by my parents. They weren't extravagant. I didn't carry a Coach purse or wear name-brand clothing. I did have a cell phone and iPod while in middle school, though. We lived in a two-story house in a nice neighborhood. Talking about money made me blush, but that's because I felt bad for people like Andrew.

Since then, the tables have turned. With the current disastrous state of the economy, talking about money makes everyone uncomfortable.

Sharing home-cooked meals instead of going out to eat is one way families can save money while enjoying each other's company.

A great number of people live on single-incomes like Andrew. But still, I couldn't relate. My family was doing fine. We no longer shopped frivolously and invested less in the shaky stock market, but other than that, nothing else was different.

Until the beginning of this year. My father got laid-off from his job. The corporation he was working for was faltering and unable to support the current number of employees. My family's income was now cut in half. It put a lot of things into perspective. I know where our priorities stand. When the decision came over whether

I should get a new car after getting my license, I knew the answer. Paying taxes, insurance, and bills was much more important than the luxury of buying something new. I happily received a used car, doing whatever I could to help my family out.

With our income cut in half, it made me appreciate things I never considered before. I was glad that my mother was such a hard-working individual who raised three children while working eight-hour days. We were lucky to have our health. After reading in the newspaper about a family where the husband and wife both lost their jobs within a year, I realized we had much to be thankful for. We had a warm home and food on our plate.

Going through a parent's lay-off is a rough experience, but strangely rewarding. It makes one realize what is important in life. It made me look at the big picture and look at those around me. This adversity and hardship built a sense of compassion and understanding.

10 Great Questions
to Ask a Guidance Counselor

1. What should I do if my adopted parents don't want me to find my birth parents?

2. How do I keep from feeling rejected if my birth parents don't want to meet me?

3. Now that my parents are divorced, I feel as if they are fighting over me. How do I keep the peace?

4. What should I do if I don't get along with my stepparent?

5. How can I let my parents know that I feel overburdened now that one of them is sick?

6. How do I stop my siblings from worrying about our parent's illness all the time?

7. What should I do if my parents can't accept the fact that I'm a member of the LGBTQ+ community?

8. What's the best way to tell my family that I no longer want to participate in religious services?

9. How can I tell my friends that I can't afford to go out every weekend without having them feel sorry for me?

10. I'm afraid we're going to lose our house because my parent is out of work. How can I ask about this without making him or her feel guilty?

The Teen Health & Wellness Personal Story Project

Be part of the Teen Health & Wellness Personal Story Project and share your story about successfully dealing with or overcoming a challenge. If your story is accepted for online publication, it will be posted on the Teen Health & Wellness site and featured on its homepage. You will also receive a certificate of achievement from Rosen Publishing and a $25 gift certificate to Barnes & Noble or Chapters.

Sharing stories is a powerful way to connect with other people. By sharing your story, you can connect with others who are dealing with these challenges. Visit www.teenhealthandwellness.com/static/personalstoryproject to read other teens' stories and to submit your own.

Scan this QR code to go to the Personal Story Project homepage.

Glossary

adolescence Teenage years; the time between puberty and adulthood.

adoption To legally make a child part of a family.

adversity A distressing and difficult set of circumstances.

custody To take legal guardianship of a child or teen, as determined by a court decision.

depression Feeling sad or unable to enjoy life as you once did for a significant period of time.

divorce The legal separation of a marriage through a court of law.

foster parent A state certified adult who provides care for a child or teen without adopting him or her.

gender identity The gender a person view themselves to be regardless of their gender assignment at birth.

layoff A temporary or permanent suspension of employment.

mortgage Payments made on a bank loan for a home.

orphanage A residential institution where children live while they are waiting to be adopted.

philanthropy Charitable giving to organizations that help humanity in some way.

sexual orientation The preference a person shows in their sexual attraction toward others.

snorkeling Swimming underwater with a diving mask and breathing tube.

transnational adoption An adoption where a child is adopted from another country.

For More Information

The Adoption Council of Canada (ACC)
416-2249 Carling Avenue
Ottawa, ON K2B 7E9
Canada
(888) 542-3678
Website: http://www.adoption.ca
Facebook: @acc.cac
Twitter @adoptioncanada
The Adoption Council of Canada (ACC) is the national
umbrella organization for adoption in Canada. It
works to raise public awareness of adoption, promote
placement of waiting children and emphasize the
importance of working with postadoption services.

Caregiver Action Network
1130 Connecticut Avenue NW, Suite 300
Washington, DC 20036-3904
(202) 454-3970
Website: http://caregiveraction.org
Facebook: @CaregiverActionNetwork
Twitter: @caregiveraction
Caregiver Action Network (CAN) is a nonprofit family
caregiver organization that aims to improve the
quality of life for Americans who care for loved
ones with chronic illness, disabilities, disease, or
who are elderly.

It Gets Better Project
110 S. Fairfax Avenue, Suite A11-71
Los Angeles, CA 90036
Website: http://www.itgetsbetter.org
Facebook: @itgetsbetter
Twitter: @itgetsbetter
The It Gets Better Project is an organization dedicated to giving LGBTQ+ youth around the world hope that life does get better. It also works to help educate society to be more understanding and accepting.

Rainbows Canada
80 Bradford Street, Suite 514
Barrie, ON L4N 6S7
Canada
(877) 403-2733
Website: http://www.rainbows.ca/default.aspx
Facebook: @rainbowscanada
Twitter: @RainbowsCanada
Rainbows Canada is an international not-for-profit organization that promotes emotional healing among children grieving a loss from a life-altering crisis, including separation, divorce, death, incarceration, and foster care.

Teen Health and Wellness
29 East 21st Street
New York, NY 10010
(877) 381-6649
Website: http://www.teenhealthandwellness.com
App: Teen Hotlines

Teen Health & Wellness provides nonjudgmental, straightforward, curricular, and self-help support on topics such as diseases, drugs and alcohol, nutrition, mental health, suicide and bullying, green living, and LGBTQ+ issues. Its free Teen Hotlines app provides a concise list of hotlines, help lines, and information lines on the subjects that affect teens most.

The Trevor Project
PO Box 69232
West Hollywood, CA 90069
West Hollywood phone: (310) 271-8845
New York phone: (212) 695-8650
Trevor Lifeline (866) 488-7386.
Email: info@thetrevorproject.org
Website: http://www.thetrevorproject.org
Facebook @TheTrevorProject
Twitter @trevorproject
The Trevor Project is an organization that provides lifesaving and life-affirming services to LGBTQ+ youth. It offers resources and a toll-free lifeline.

United States Department of Labor
200 Constitution Avenue NW
Washington, DC 20210
(866) 487-2365
Website: http://www.dol.gov
Facebook: @departmentoflabor
Twitter: @USDOL
The United States Department of Labor is the department of the US federal government responsible

for occupational safety, wage and hour standards, unemployment insurance benefits, reemployment, and related issues. The department also offers information on job trends.

Websites

Because of the changing nature of internet links, Rosen Publishing has developed an online list of websites related to the subject of this book. This site is updated regularly. Please use this link to access this list:

http://www.rosenlinks.com/TNV/Family

For Further Reading

Baker, Amy J. L., PhD, and Katherine C. Andre, PhD. *Getting Through My Parents' Divorce: A Workbook for Children Coping with Divorce, Parental Alienation, and Loyalty Conflicts*. Oakland, CA: Instant Help Books, 2015.

Callahan, Timothy. *A Teen's Guide to Custody* (Divorce and Your Family). New York, NY: Rosen Publishing, 2017.

Desetta, Al, ed. *Pressure: True Stories by Teens About Stress* (Real Teen Voices Series). Golden Valley, MN: Free Spirit Publishing, 2012.

Huegel, Kelly. *GLBTQ: The Survival Guide for Gay, Lesbian, Bisexual, Transgender, and Questioning Teens*. Minneapolis, MN: Free Spirit Publishing, Inc., 2014.

Jewell, Jeremy D. *Teen Survival Guide to Parent Divorce or Separation: A Teen First Self-Guided Workbook*. Champaign, IL: Research Press, 2015.

Jones, Viola, and Tabitha Wainwright. *Living with an Illness in the Family* (Family Issues and You). New York, NY: Rosen Publishing, 2016.

Leahy, Robert L. *Keeping Your Head After Losing Your Job: How to Survive Unemployment*. Lake Forest, CA: Behler Publications, 2013.

Lenarki, Becky. *Understanding Your Parents' Divorce* (Divorce and Your Family). New York, NY: Rosen Publishing, 2017.

Mooney, Carla. *Comparative Religion: Investigate the World Through Religious Tradition* (Inquire and

Investigate). White River Junction, VT: Nomad Press, 2015.

Morrow, Paula. *My Parents Are Divorcing. Now What?* (Teen Life 411). New York, NY: Rosen Publishing, 2015.

Slade, Suzanne Buckingham. *Adopted: The Ultimate Teen Guide* (It Happened to Me). Lanham, MD: Scarecrow Press, Inc. 2013.

Testa, Rylan Jay, et al. *The Gender Quest Workbook: A Guide for Teens and Young Adults Exploring Gender Identity*. Oakland, CA: Instant Help Books. 2015.

Bibliography

"Allison's Story." Teen Health and Wellness, October 2016. http://www.teenhealthandwellness.com /article/359/12/allisons-story.

Ananat, Elizabeth Oltmans. "How Job Loss Affects Youngsters and their Schools." Scholars Strategy Network, May 2012. http://www .scholarsstrategynetwork.org/brief/ how-job-losses-affect-youngsters-and-their-schools.

"Arlene's Story." Teen Health and Wellness, June 2015. http://www.teenhealthandwellness.com/article/257/7 /arlenes-story.

"Brielle's Story." Teen Health and Wellness, March 2016. http://www.teenhealthandwellness.com/article/352/7 /brielles-story.

"Brittany's Story." Teen Health and Wellness, June 2015. http://www.teenhealthandwellness.com/article/353/7 /brittanys-story.

"Christina's Story." Teen Health and Wellness, October 2016. http://www.teenhealthandwellness.com /article/359/8/christinas-story.

Family & Youth Services Bureau. "Supportive Families Make a Difference for Lesbian, Gay, Bisexual and Transgender Youth." Retrieved March 25, 2017. https://ncfy.acf.hhs.gov/features/serving-lesbian-gay -bisexual-transgender-and-questioning-youth-open -arms/supportive.

"Gabriella's Story." Teen Health and Wellness, October 2016. http://www.teenhealthandwellness.com /article/112/6/gabriellas-story.

Gaspard, Terry, MSW, LICSW. "Four Ways to Help Your Teenage Daughter Cope with Divorce." Huffington Post, September 2013. http://www.huffingtonpost .com/terry-gaspard-msw-licsw/4-ways-to-help-your -teena_b_3241284.html.

Herman, Abby. "Co-parenting Across State Lines," *Solo Parent Magazine*, May 6, 2015. http://soloparentmag .com/co-parenting-across-state-lines.

"Libby's Story." Teen Health and Wellness, October 2016. http://www.teenhealthandwellness.com /article/112/8/libbys-story.

"Matthew's Story." Teen Health and Wellness, October 2016. http://www.teenhealthandwellness.com /article/506/10/matthews-story.

Melson, Gail F, PhD. "Parents Lose Jobs, and Children Suffer: Unemployment Is a Child Welfare Issue." *Psychology Today*, January 22, 2014. https://www .psychologytoday.com/blog/why-the-wild-things- are/201401/parents-lose-jobs-and-children-suffer.

"Monica's Story." Teen Health and Wellness, March 2017. http://www.teenhealthandwellness.com /article/60/10/monicas-story.

National Cancer Institute. "Teens Who Have a Family Member with Cancer." Retrieved March 25, 2017. https://www.cancer.gov/about-cancer/coping /caregiver-support/teens.

Pickhard, Carl E. PhD. "How Parental Divorce Can Impact Adolescence Now and Later." *Psychology Today*, November 2015. https://www.psychologytoday.com /blog/surviving-your-childs-adolescence/201511/how -parental-divorce-can-impact-adolescence-now-and.

"Rebecca's Story." Teen Health and Wellness, March 2017. http://www.teenhealthandwellness.com /article/60/9/rebeccas-story.

Riley, Debbie, LCMFT. "6 Questions Every Adopted Teen Wants Answered." Adoptive Families. Retrieved March 25, 2017. https://www.adoptivefamilies.com /parenting/questions-adopted-teen-wants-answered.

Russell, Wendy Thomas, "10 Commandments for Talking to Your Kids About Religion," *PBS News Hour*, March 31, 2015. http://www.pbs.org/newshour /updates/10-commandments-talking-kids-religion.

Shaw, Gina. "Coming Out as a LGBT Teen: Should You Come Out as a LGBT Teen? Whom Might You Tell, and How?" WebMD. Retrieved March 25, 2017. http://teens.webmd.com/features /coming-out-as-lgbt-teen.

Index

M

P

R

S

T

About the Editor

Jennifer Landau is an author and editor who has written about psychological bullying, cybercitizenship, and drug and alcohol abuse, among other topics. She has an MA in English from New York University and an MST in general and special education from Fordham University. Landau has taught writing to young children, teens, and seniors.

About Dr. Jan

Dr. Jan Hittelman, a licensed psychologist with over thirty years experience working with children and families, has authored monthly columns for the *Daily Camera*, Boulder Valley School District, and online for Rosen Publishing Group. He is the founder of the Boulder Counseling Cooperative and the director of Boulder Psychological Services.

Photo Credits

Cover, pp. 6, 17 Monkey Business/Shutterstock.com; p. 5 Boston Globe/Getty Images; p. 10 Dragos Asaftei/Shutterstock.com; p. 13 © iStockphoto.com/Dmbaker; p. 14 Jupiterimages/PHOTOS.com/Thinkstock; p. 19 SpeedKingz/Shutterstock.com; p. 22 Andrew Bret Wallis/Photodisc/Getty Images; p. 23 Air Images/Shutterstock .com; p. 26 Design Pics/Thinkstock; p. 28 Creatas Images/Creatas/Thinkstock; p. 31 ERproductions Ltd/Blend Images/Getty Images; p. 34 Boston Globe/Getty Images; p. 36 Ira Block/NATIONAL GEOGRAPHIC IMAGE COLLECTION/Getty Images; p. 39 Vitchanan Photography/Shutterstock.com; p. 41 Rawpixel.com/Shutterstock .com; p. 43 Hero Images/Getty Images; p. 45 IPGGutenbergUKLtd /iStock/Thinkstock; p. 48 India Picture/Shutterstock.com; interior pages graphic elements natt/Shutterstock.com.

Design and Layout: Nicole Russo-Duca; Photo Research: Sherri Jackson